INTERNATIONAL
ADOPTION

INTERNATIONAL
ADOPTION

BY REBECCA FELIX

CONTENT CONSULTANT
CYNTHIA R. MABRY
PROFESSOR, HOWARD UNIVERSITY
SCHOOL OF LAW

Essential Library

An Imprint of Abdo Publishing | www.abdopublishing.com

www.abdopublishing.com

Published by Abdo Publishing, a division of ABDO, PO Box 398166, Minneapolis, Minnesota 55439. Copyright © 2015 by Abdo Consulting Group, Inc. International copyrights reserved in all countries. No part of this book may be reproduced in any form without written permission from the publisher. Essential Library™ is a trademark and logo of Abdo Publishing.

Printed in the United States of America, North Mankato, Minnesota
042014
092014

**THIS BOOK CONTAINS
RECYCLED MATERIALS**

Cover Photo: Thinkstock
Interior Photos: Thinkstock, 2; Nunnicha Supagrit/Alamy, 6; Bryan Smith/Zuma Press/ Corbis, 9; Moises Castillo/AP Images, 17, 44; James Matenhoff/AP Images, 18; Ernest K. Bennett/AP Images, 23; Bettmann/Corbis, 26; Isabel Ellsen/Corbis, 29; Philippe Wojazer/Reuters/Corbis, 31; David Edwards/National Geographic Image Collection/ Glow Images, 32; Twonix Studio/Shutterstock Images, 36; Red Line Editorial, 39, 54; Sandra Sebastián/epa/Corbis, 43; Stringer/Imaginechina/AP Images, 49; Michele Westmorland/Corbis, 56; Patrik Giardino/Corbis, 61; Heng Sinith/AP Images, 63; Daily Mail/Rex/Alamy, 66; Amanda Koster/Corbis, 71; Lynn Johnson/National Geographic Image Collection/Glow Images, 73; Misha Japaridze/AP Images, 74; iStockphoto/Thinkstock, 80; Alyaksandr Stzhalkouski/Alamy, 85; Hannah Mentz/ Corbis, 86; Imaginechina/Corbis, 89; Koji Sasahar/AP Images, 95

Editor: Susan E. Hamen
Series Designer: Becky Daum

Library of Congress Control Number: 2014932563

Cataloging-in-Publication Data

Felix, Rebecca.
International adoption / Rebecca Felix.
p. cm. -- (Essential issues)
Includes bibliographical references and index.
ISBN 978-1-62403-420-6
1. Intercountry adoption--Juvenile literature. 2. Adoption--Juvenile literature. 3. Adopted children--Juvenile literature. I. Title.
362.734--dc23

2014932563

CONTENTS

CHAPTER
ONE

IN NEED OF A HOME

In the summer of 2000, an infant was found in a market in Shaoyang, China. She was just 13 days old. Found on her was a handwritten note with the name Shao Zhi Ying scrawled upon it. The police put an ad in the paper searching for Shao Zhi Ying's mother. Doing so was standard protocol for this type of occurrence, which happened frequently. As expected, no one came forward. Shao Zhi Ying's mother had abandoned her at a market, knowing someone was likely to find her.

Opportunity Overseas

Zhi Ying was taken to an orphanage. But she would have little chance of being adopted in China. The country's one-child policy meant many homes legally did not have room to take in an abandoned or orphaned child. This policy may have been the reason Zhi Ying's mother left her in the first place. Her sex made her abandonment

Strict laws regarding family size in China lead to a number of baby girls being abandoned every year.

even more predictable. Belief in Confucianism is widespread in China. The religion stresses the importance of family bloodlines being carried through male offspring. This ideology creates a strong preference for biological males to fulfill a Chinese family's one-child quota.

Across the globe, in Brooklyn, New York, a woman named Laura received a call sharing the news of Zhi Ying's abandonment. Laura was hoping to adopt a child from China and had filed paperwork to begin the process. Nine months later, she brought Zhi Ying, whom she renamed Cydney, home.

Today, 13-year-old Cydney is thriving in New York. She attends a world-renowned performing and music arts high school where she studies singing. She is well adjusted and adored by her adoptive mother. Cydney's adoption experience is typical for the majority of children adopted internationally. But for some children, their adoption causes greater difficulties.

Misled Abroad

In the autumn of 2006, three sisters had been living a new life for several weeks. The young girls had made what they believed was a temporary move from Ethiopia

Successful international adoptions give children loving homes.

to New Mexico. The sisters were to get an education during their stay in the United States and then return to Ethiopia—and their family there—with a bright future ahead.

Life in the United States involved many changes, including a new language, a new climate, and new living situations. The sisters were also given new names. Thirteen-year old Tarikuwa was renamed Journee. Yemisrach, 11 years old, became Meya. The youngest, six-year-old Tseganesh, became Maree. New names were the first of many upsetting surprises. Others included being asked to call the adult male they lived with "Dad." This confused the girls because their father was in Ethiopia. The biggest shock came when the eldest asked when she and her sisters would be going home to Ethiopia. They were told never—their move had been permanent.

Lies and Legality

The three sisters had been internationally adopted without realizing it. They were devastated. The girls begged to go home and grieved for their family.

Their adoptive mother, Katie, and her husband, Calvin, were just as distraught. Just as the sisters were lied to by the organizations facilitating the exchange, telling them their move was temporary and centered on an education, so were Katie and Calvin misled. They were told a sad—and untrue—backstory of the girls' lives in Ethiopia: the girls' mother died of AIDS and their father was HIV positive and dying. The three sisters had no other family and would be forced to turn to prostitution in order to earn money to be able to survive on their own in Ethiopia. In reality, the girls' mother had died in childbirth, but their father was healthy. He and the girls' other family in Ethiopia were just as blindsided by the truth of the exchange. Years of turmoil plagued the biological and adoptive families as legal obstacles kept the adoption from being dissolved. Their experience is rare, but it is not unique. And it demonstrates only one of the issues related to international adoption today.

What Is International Adoption?

International adoption is the adoption of children from one country into another. It is also called intercountry adoption. Children and their adoptive parents are often of a different ethnicity, race, culture, and class. They may speak different languages. International adoptions typically consist of children being adopted from poorer or less-developed nations into more-developed or wealthy nations. Tens of thousands of children from countries such as China, Russia, Guatemala, and Ethiopia have been adopted by American parents, who adopt half of all internationally adopted children.[2]

Positives of international adoption include removing child refugees from danger, oppression, or the chaos and aftermath of war or natural disaster. It can also increase an adopting family and community's exposure to and tolerance of other cultures. Adopting parents add a beloved child to their families. International adoption can also provide relief to developing nations that lack the resources to adequately care for orphans.

Advocates and opponents of international adoption alike agree adoption is better than a child becoming institutionalized. This occurs when a child lives for an extended period of time in an institution, usually a hospital or orphanage, and suffers emotional, mental, and physical delays and disorders as a result of the lack of stimulation, love, and interaction they would find in a family setting. Children older than five and children with disabilities or illnesses are in the greatest danger of being left in institutions.

An overwhelming number of international adoptions are successful and legal. But sometimes adoptions that appear legal and successful—where the adopted child is loved, cared for, and happy—have dark, hidden backstories. And sometimes adoptions bring additional trauma to the adopted children.

Corruption and Controversy

In recent years, reports have emerged of children—especially healthy infants and toddlers—who have been taken from biological parents through deception, coercion, or kidnapping, and are then adopted abroad, never to see their families again. Sometimes the process of international adoption can begin to resemble child trafficking. These unethical practices stem from the great demand for international adoptions and the large

CHILD TRAFFICKING

Child trafficking is the commoditization of children. Commoditization is turning something that is not a good or a service into a commodity, or something that can be bought and sold. Children who are trafficked are treated as merchandise, exported or imported across borders. Children can be trafficked for purposes of adoption, but also for forced labor, sexual slavery or prostitution, and even for the harvesting of their organs for use in transplants. The person controlling trafficking systems receives payment for the process. Individuals who are trafficked are tricked, lied to, or forced to comply. The United Nations International Children's Emergency Fund (UNICEF) estimates more than 1 million children are trafficked each year. Human trafficking creates the world's second-largest illegal income, after drug trafficking.[3]

amounts of money exchanged for adoption processing fees. The lure of money can lead to corruption, especially in poorer countries.

Parents have been misled, told their children are going to the United States to receive an education and can return to their country of origin anytime they would like, when it is not true. The children are instead adopted into families who are also misinformed about the children's history and family.

Some opponents of international adoption claim taking a child out of his or her birth culture also strips from the child the right to a cultural identity. Opponents also argue children are important resources of developing nations, a nation's future leaders, entrepreneurs, and inventors. Therefore removing young

"The emotional nature of intercountry adoption often leads each side to demonize the other, impeding the ability to find common ground. Moreover, keeping the debate focused on whether intercountry adoption is good or bad is problematic; there will always be compelling arguments on either side, and compelling reasons to which each can point in support of their position. As such, focusing on the positives or negatives in the debate amounts to a stand-off in which neither side is willing to compromise any ground, a perpetual lose-lose situation."[4]
—Jena Martin, author of The Good, The Bad, and The Ugly: The New Way of Looking at the Intercountry Adoption Debate

generations and dispersing them abroad strips the birth countries of their future.

Family law and international child law professor Judith Masson says some opponents also believe international adoption creates problems for domestic adoption systems. In countries receiving foreign children, the older or disabled children up for domestic adoption may stand a lower chance of being adopted when young, healthy foreign children are available.

Other problems exist as well. Controversy surrounding international adoption has led to stricter regulations, which makes completing international adoption more difficult. Children therefore remain in institutions longer, increasing their risk of developing mental, behavioral, or physical effects. Some adoptive parents have claimed adoption facilitators do not prepare parents for these effects or other special needs, or even hide these issues from parents during the adoption process. Furthermore, orphanages often lack previous medical information for children who are abandoned, and therefore are unable to provide a thorough medical history to adoptive parents.

Some adoptive parents who were not prepared or did not desire to raise children with special needs or behavioral issues have responded by "re-homing" these children. In re-homing, adoptive parents who no longer want to care for their adopted child find another family willing to take the adopted child without formal paperwork. It is painful for the discarded children and can place them in dangerous situations of abuse. Re-homing is controversial and illegal, and it has risen in recent years.

Three Sides

If international adoptions create so much controversy, why not just stop them altogether? Cases of corruption and abuse have caused many countries to do just that, and international adoptions have been declining in recent years. But while halting adoptions could be the answer to corruption and abuse, it is not a solution that prevents institutionalization or helps children living in poverty, hunger, or in a state of war. To shut down all international adoptions would take away the opportunity of finding a family from children who may have no other chance.

International adoption is a complex issue with more than two sides. As Masson puts it, international adoption creates a debate between three sides: "abolitionists,

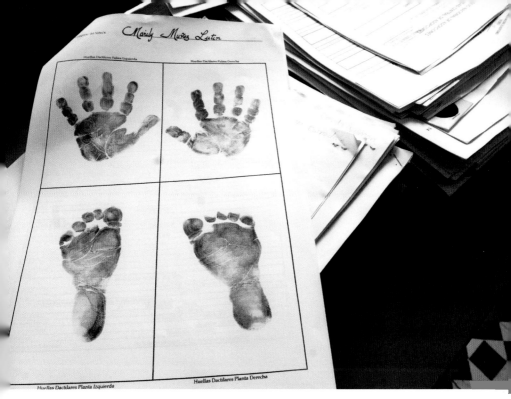

Experts disagree on the future of international adoption and how it affects the adopted children.

pragmatists, and promoters."[5] Abolitionists, Masson says, focus on negative aspects of international adoption and want to stop them altogether. Pragmatists believe in incorporating better regulations to improve standards and stop corruption and abuse of the system. Promoters believe in providing a safe environment and family to children in need wherever they are from, whatever the cost. Those on all sides have recognized the need to establish a stronger framework addressing and preventing issues across a broad worldwide scope, while ultimately keeping children's well-being in focus.

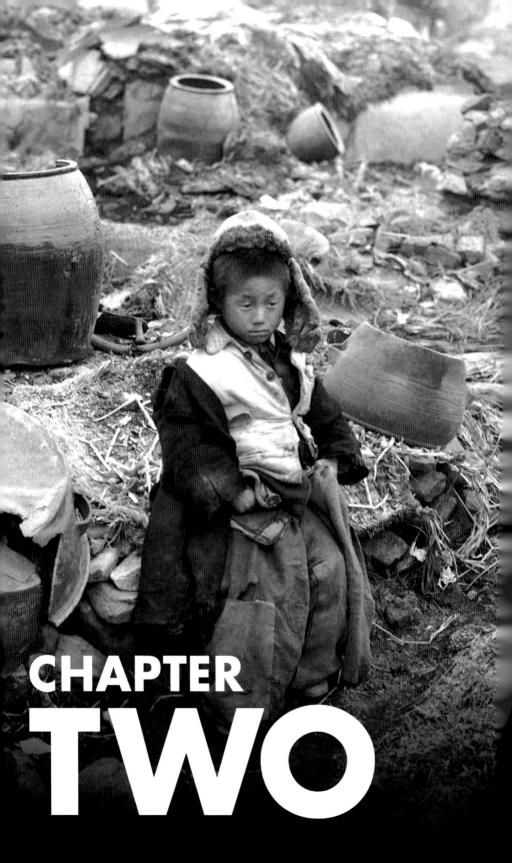

CHAPTER
TWO

HISTORY OF INTERNATIONAL ADOPTION

International adoption is a relatively new concept. Large-scale international adoptions began in the 1940s, and it is estimated more than 950,000 children have been internationally adopted since then.[1] The first major waves of international adoption in the mid-1900s grew from humanitarian efforts to assist children from countries devastated by war or natural disaster. The desire to provide children with a family and home and remove them from institutions, poverty, political conflict, or epidemics spurred later adoptions. International adoptions rose into the 1980s, increased in the 1990s, and peaked in 2004. Since then, a steady decline has occurred in the number of international adoptions. Experts attribute this decline to sending countries being wary of controversies surrounding

Wars often leave children parentless. Many times, these war orphans are sent from their homelands and are adopted internationally.

international adoption and the stricter regulations that have developed because of these controversies. Much of this history involves the United States; until 2009, it received approximately half of all international adoptions worldwide.[2]

War Rescue

The first major waves of interest in international adoption occurred following the end of World War II (1939–1945). A political initiative went into effect to rebuild countries devastated by war. Rather than providing aid to war orphans in their home countries, including Germany and Japan, the children were airlifted to the United States for adoption. According to John Seabrook of the *New Yorker* magazine, the media depicted these operations as saving the foreign child in need, an image by then already ingrained in American culture. But, he said, the operations were also a political demonstration of goodwill toward developing nations and a display of the United States' power.

The idea of rescuing children expanded to include means other than physical adoption and relocation. Organizations urged Americans to participate in moral and monetary adoptions of foreign children, which

MORAL AND MONETARY ADOPTIONS

In December 1946, the United Nations International Children's Emergency Fund (UNICEF) was created to aid European children suffering from hunger or disease in the aftermath of the war. UNICEF employed the same tactics political figures had, marketing photos of hungry children abroad. These efforts solidified the imagery of how "hunger" or being in "need" was interpreted in US culture. The images of children in crises also stirred the humanitarian impulses of several religious groups, which campaigned for and facilitated monetary adoptions as well.

Four years after World War II, US writer Norman Cousins suggested Americans make a "moral adoption" of Japanese children who were made orphans by US bombs dropped on Japan during the war. Due to political animosity between the two nations leading up to and in the aftermath of the bombings, Japanese people were not allowed to immigrate to the United States at the time. Therefore, Japanese children adopted as Cousins suggested would continue living in Japan, but they would take on the last name of the Americans who morally adopted them and have all their needs paid for by their adoptive parents.

involved sending financial support for a child overseas instead of taking a child into their home. Providing humanitarian rescue through physical removal remained popular, however, and grew in the wake of other political conflicts.

Korean War

When Japanese rule ended in Korea at the end of World War II, feelings of national pride erupted. Full-blooded Koreans were idealized and those of mixed blood were shunned, including children of unmarried Korean women and US soldiers. The Korean War (1950–1953) also left behind a number of war orphans, including children fathered by US soldiers. Domestic adoptions of these multiracial children were socially discouraged. The stage was set for a second major wave of international adoption.

In 1954, the Christian organization World Visions created a documentary featuring children in orphanages in South Korea, and it aired in churches across the United States. The video made a lasting impact on Oregon couple Bertha and Henry Holt—who in turn changed the future landscape of international adoption.

A group of 89 Korean orphans coordinated by the Holts arrived in San Francisco in December 1956.

The Holts

The Holts initially sent monetary support to South Korea. But soon, deeply affected by the video and proclaiming God sent them a message, they decided to adopt eight South Korean orphans. Harry successfully lobbied Congress to create a special act to allow him to adopt the eight children, as regulations at the time only allowed the adoption of two.

The arrival of the eight children created a media sensation. The Holts became famous. With their newfound fame, the couple urged other Americans to open their hearts and homes to Korean orphans, whom the Holts hoped would become Christians. The Holts received thousands of adoption and sponsoring requests, and children were flown from South Korea to the United States, sometimes as many as 100 at a time. The Holts founded Holt International Children's Services in 1956.

Some practices Holt International followed in earlier days would be controversial today, such as adopting on behalf of parents who were denied domestic US adoptions, working only with Christian couples—a sign today that evangelization is a priority—and participating in what author Kathryn Joyce calls "order-taking," or hunting for adoptive children who match the physical features desired by the adoptive parents.[3] Despite this, Holt International facilitated many adoptions and had an immense influence on the development and growth of international adoption. It grew into one of the longest-running and largest international adoption agencies in the country and still operates today.

Growing Trend, Corruption Concerns

Worldwide, it is estimated more than 50,000 children were adopted internationally between 1948 and 1969. In addition to the United States, receiving countries and regions included the Netherlands, Belgium, Scandinavia, Denmark, and other European nations.[4] In the 1970s, following the Vietnam War (1954–1975), the trend of airlifting children from areas of conflict continued.

In the aftermath of these airlifts, some members of US society and media expected the children would feel grateful and happy about their new lives, culture, names, and families—happy to be out of the chaos or poverty of their home country. But some adopted children resented being torn from their homeland and having new lives thrust upon them. Many struggled to fit in as they grew up in the United States and felt they did not belong. Being airlifted from chaos and so quickly submerged in a new place and culture

VIETNAM WAR: OPERATION BABYLIFT

When the Vietnam War ended in 1975, US President Gerald Ford announced a directive called Operation Babylift. US adoption organizations, including Holt International, aided military units in flying approximately 2,700 children from Vietnamese orphanages to the United States and approximately 1,300 to Canada.[5]

Operation Babylift created controversy and drew heavy criticism, however, as not all children airlifted were confirmed orphans. Some had missing or unclear background information, and very likely still had living parents or family in Vietnam. There were suspicions that some of the children may have been taken right from the streets and shipped abroad.

War orphans from Vietnam were loaded onto cargo planes and flown to the Philippines for medical screenings and then on to the United States during Operation Babylift.

created confusion. The airlift operations also implied the countries the children were removed from were inferior and that US culture was better.

A significant rise in international adoptions occurred from 1980 to 1986. In the 1980s, unrest from civil wars in Latin American and African countries influenced international adoptions. With an increasing demand for children from Latin America, corruption broke out. Children were bought or kidnapped. Sometimes military forces killed people rebelling against the government and then sold their children for international adoption. Pressure on legal systems to better regulate and handle issues emerged as international adoption spread, leading to the creation of multinational agreements and guidelines in the coming years.

By 1989, the number of countries sending out children for adoption grew from 22 to 63.[6] In the early 1990s, one country emerged as a top sending country, and remains so today.

Legal Legacy: China

In the late 1970s, China's fast-growing population neared 1 billion people.[7] In 1980, the Chinese government instituted a nationwide one-child policy to curb overpopulation. Those who did not comply with the law faced fines, or in some cases were forced into abortions or sterilization. This policy led to widespread abandonment of children by families who wanted to avoid violating the policy.

ABANDONED CHINESE GIRLS

Historically, the majority of abandoned children in China have been girls. In addition to the belief that bloodlines carry on through male offspring, male children also carry on the family name and inherit family land in China.

Despite this preference, research proved childless Chinese families were not unwilling to adopt abandoned girls. However, a 1991 law made domestic adoption in China difficult. The new law said adoptive parents in China had to be childless and over the age of 35. This age was considered unacceptably old to become a parent in Chinese society. The result was an increase in children up for adoption and a decrease of eligible Chinese adoptive families.

Girls especially were abandoned due to the culture's preference for boys.

The Chinese government sought international adoptions as a solution for dealing with the increasing number of abandoned children filling orphanages. More than 125,000 children were adopted from China into foreign homes between 1992 and 2010.[8]

Legal Legacy: Romania

Following the fall of communism in Eastern Europe in 1989, international adoptions from this region increased. Romania's Communist dictator, Nicolae Ceaușescu, was overthrown and executed in 1989 after a 24-year rule. Ceaușescu made birth control illegal in order to increase Romania's working population. Women who did not already have several children were banned from having abortions.

Ceaușescu's economic decisions smothered Romania's economy, and parents struggled to provide for their growing families in the weakening economy. Orphanages with unsafe and unhealthy conditions filled with children. These children often lived in filth, without interaction or even room to move, and suffered developmental delays and disorders because

Reporters discovered children in Romanian orphanages in the late 1980s living in horrific conditions.

of it. The grim circumstances in these orphanages were revealed by televised reports that aired after Ceaușescu's assassination, to the horror of shocked audiences. Approximately 10,000 adoptions from Romania followed in 1990 and 1991.[9]

Epidemics and Natural Disasters

In the 1990s and 2000s, Africa became a significant region of origin for international adoptions. Removing children from poverty and epidemics was a driving force behind this shift.

During these decades, an epidemic of the virus HIV, which causes AIDS, broke out in several African countries. The AIDS crisis created many orphans. In other cases, adults who were too sick to work could not support their children. International adoption advocates argued that while international adoption was not a permanent solution to the spread of AIDS in the region, it could be a temporary solution until the core problem could be resolved. Removing the children would save them from possible infection when they became adults and would lessen the economic crisis. Adopting from Africa also became popular as American celebrities completing adoptions drew publicity.

In January 2010, an earthquake hit Haiti and caused major devastation. Similar to the situation following the 2004 earthquake and tsunami in the Indian Ocean, towns were demolished, the government stopped functioning, families were torn apart, and many children became orphans. Immediately following the disaster, international adoptions for Haitian children that had been pending were speeded up to remove the children from the chaos. This rushed process created major controversy as critics wondered whether facilitators were taking the time to ensure children being adopted were in fact orphans and not just separated from their parents. Adoption controversy soon overshadowed the natural disaster itself in the media.

Following a disastrous earthquake in Haiti, orphans were adopted to families in several countries, including the United States, Canada, and France.

Responding to reports of corruption in the wake of the Haiti earthquake, the US Adoptees of Color Roundtable, a group of adults who were adopted from abroad as children, released a statement on the controversial history of international adoption. "For more than fifty years, 'orphaned children' have been shipped from areas of war, natural disasters, and poverty to supposedly better lives in Europe and North America," it read. "We seek to challenge those who abuse the phrase 'Every child deserves a family' to rethink how this phrase is used to justify the removal of children."[10]

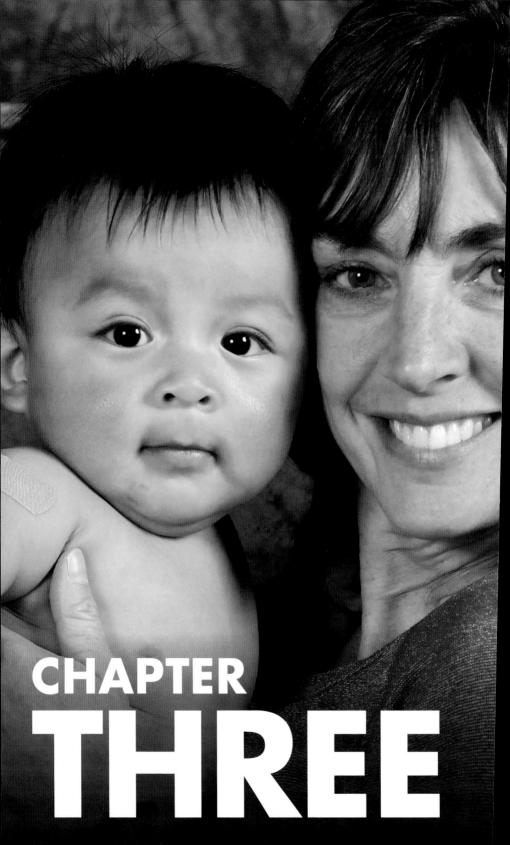

CHAPTER THREE

ADOPTERS AND ADOPTEES

D etermining typical characteristics of adopters and adoptees is a difficult task. A worldwide 2009 United Nations study reported only approximately half of the countries that allow data about international adoption to be published actually share it. North America is the only region where all countries publish at least some data on the subject.

Who Adopts Internationally?

According to the 2009 UN study, most adoptive parents are between the ages of 30 and 44. Many sending countries have adoptive parent age requirements, so this age likely reflects the minimums and maximums for the countries that have data.[1]

Adoptive parents who are older, members of same-sex couples, single, disabled, recovering from a serious illness, or even overweight are sometimes labeled

Criteria for adoptive parents have changed over the years, making it possible for single parents and same-sex couples to adopt in some places.

"special needs" parents. They may not be allowed to adopt from countries with complex restrictions. On the other hand, if these parents do not meet standards in a particular country, there are many others to look into.

Adoptive parents must also complete and pass a home study before adopting a child from abroad to ensure their background, lifestyle, and home setting are suitable for raising a child. Meeting the requirements of international adoption is just the first step in a long process.

Choosing Adoption

Some people choose adoption—either domestic or international—when becoming pregnant through traditional or assisted reproductive methods proves to

UN ADOPTION STUDY

In 2009, the United Nations (UN) published a study by the Population Division of the Department of Economic and Social Affairs of the United Nations Secretariat that focused on adoption. It was the first study of its kind ever done by the organization. At the time, 173 countries allowed adoption. The study found 128 countries publish information on adoptions, and only 88 made distinctions between domestic and international adoption data. An additional nine countries published information specifically on international adoption only.[2] The study concluded the lack of complete information makes it difficult to compare statistics and data on international adoptions worldwide.

be difficult or impossible. Others choose to adopt rather than add to the world's ever-expanding population. Some parents choose adoption because they were adopted themselves or because they are sympathetic to children in orphanages or foster homes and want to provide them a home. Many adoptive parents already have biological children. There are fewer children, especially infants, available for domestic adoption in the United States and other wealthy, developed nations. Growing social acceptance of younger, unwed mothers, more easily available contraception, couples marrying later in life, and improved access to welfare has enabled more biological mothers to keep their children. Also, fewer teenagers are becoming pregnant. But the demand for adoptable children has remained high in the United States for decades. This imbalance creates heavy competition with other adoptive parents when a child does become available domestically, causing some prospective parents to seek children abroad instead.

In the United States, in many cases biological mothers choose the adoptive parents they place their children with. Prospective adoptive parents create a profile and basically advertise for biological mothers to choose them. Many adoptive parents do not like this

Open adoption allows a birth mother to choose the adoptive parents for her baby. Sometimes, the birth mother maintains contact with the adoptive family.

process. Others feel there are too many children in need of homes around the world for two sets of parents to compete for one child.

In some domestic adoptions in the United States, adopting parents must allow the child to have lifelong contact with one or both biological parents. Some adoptive parents fear the biological parents might change their minds at any time during the child's life and work to overturn the adoption. There is a much lower chance of this happening in international adoption, where the biological family is across the globe. US biological mothers are not bound legally to any adoption documents signed before giving birth. Additionally, state laws provide the biological mother with a time period after birth to change her mind about the adoption.

Adoptive parents may also seek international adoption because they feel they are rescuing a child from a foreign orphanage they believe has worse conditions than a US institution. Other motives to adopt internationally include cultural curiosity, ties, or admiration. Some adoptive parents adopt from a country associated with their ethnicity, where they have ancestors or living relatives, or where they have traveled or spent time living. Adoptive parents may also choose international adoption to build a diverse family or because they admire a certain culture and want to expose themselves and their family to it. Some want to adopt to make a statement socially on blending cultures.

International Adoptee Demographics

A 2009 study by the UN published statistics from 27 countries on the age of children adopted internationally. The median age of those children was 4.4 years old. In most countries, less than half of the children adopted were under one year old. The countries with the highest percentage of infants adopted into the country were Australia, Ireland, and the United States, each with 40 percent or more of the children adopted from abroad at less than one year old.[3] In the United States, children under one year old made up 40 percent or more of international adoptions between the years 1999 and 2007.[4] In 2013, the US Department of State reported 58 percent of the total children adopted from overseas into the United States in the past year were between one and four years old and 24 percent were between five and twelve years old.[5]

Some countries place age maximums on adopted children, determining children in their later teens too old to adopt. Others allow adults to be adopted internationally if they give consent. In some countries, children can consent to or deny their own adoption. Depending on the country, the youngest age a child can be to reject their adoption ranges from 10 to 14 years.

A higher percentage of the children who are adopted from abroad today have special needs. A 2013 report by the Donaldson Adoption Institute found 47 percent of adoptive parents in the United States adopted a child from abroad who had special needs, although less than 25 percent of adoptive parents planned to.[6] Historically,

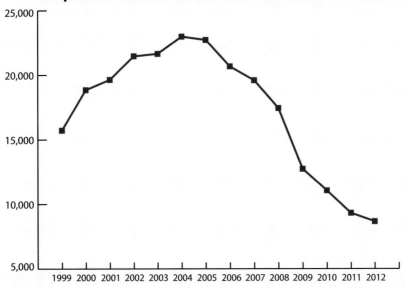

Adopted Children Received in the United States 1999–2012

more girls have been adopted worldwide than boys. This may be because of some countries' cultural tendencies to abandon female children.

Why Do Biological Parents Place Their Children for Adoption?

Orphans are placed for adoption because they do not have living parents to care for them. Living parents place their children for adoption for several reasons.

In some cultures, having a child out of wedlock or raising a child as a single parent is discouraged or not socially acceptable. Shame leads biological mothers to place their children for adoption. Teen pregnancy, failed contraception, pregnancy as the result of rape, and laws against abortion or contraception also contribute to mothers placing their children for adoption.

Not all parents who place their children for adoption want to. Economics can also influence a parent's decision. When parents struggle to feed and clothe their children, they may place them in an orphanage as a temporary or permanent solution. Some parents view orphanages as a temporary boardinghouse and retain contact with their children living there. But some of these children are placed for adoption even if their parents had not intended it.

Deceit, Sales, and Filling Orphanages

While lack of sufficient data makes it difficult for experts to say with certainty how common purposeful or accidental deceit is, many agree it contributes to the number of children placed in international adoptions. The terms used to describe children eligible for adoption can be misinterpreted, used differently in different cultures, or skewed by the media. Investigative journalist E. J. Graff cited UNICEF for creating widespread confusion of the term *orphan* in 2006: "UNICEF reported an estimated 132 million orphans in sub-Saharan Africa, Asia, Latin America, and the Caribbean. But the organization's definition of 'orphan' includes children who have lost just one parent, either to desertion or death. Just 10 percent of the total—13 million children—have lost both parents, and most of these live with extended family."[7] Purposeful or accidental confusion of terms occurs on smaller scales as well, within interactions between birth families, facilitators, and adoptive parents. In the Western world, it is understood that adoption is a permanent change of family where adoptive parents take over all legal aspects of parenting. Adoption is not understood or interpreted this way around the world, however. Some countries do not have the concept of adoption in their culture. Former US Embassy employee Freda Luzinda spent two working years in Uganda

BIRTH MOTHERS SEND ABROAD

In recent years, a growing number of US birth mothers have chosen foreign parents, often from Canada and the Netherlands, to adopt their children. Nearly all of the US children adopted by parents in foreign countries are African American or mixed-race African Americans, according to attorneys facilitating the exchanges. Some mothers fear their children will face discrimination in the United States and so choose parents overseas, living in countries the biological parents perceive as more open-minded. Some children from the US welfare system have been adopted internationally, too, especially in Canada.

and said the local language Luganda does not have a word meaning *adoption*. Adoption facilitators may accidentally or purposefully mislead or lie to biological parents when accepting their children into an orphanage or adoption program. Poor families are sometimes coerced or tricked into signing up their children, told the child will gain a Western education and return home with skills and money. Some biological mothers in Guatemala received money when they placed their children for adoption. Women who needed money felt pressured to give up their children. A small number became pregnant to make money from selling a baby.

Some people argue demand is the reason a majority of children are up for international adoption. In countries experiencing economic crisis, orphanages fill because poor parents see them as a way to support their children. Adoption agencies point out to prospective parents the high number of children in orphanages in a certain area, suggesting that adoption is needed there.

In 2011, Guatemalan mothers who claim their children were adopted illegally protested against reopening Guatemala for international adoption.

This creates interest and demand. More orphanages are built to supply this demand and children are found to fill them. As Doug Webb of UNICEF said, "If you build an orphanage, it will be filled with kids."[9] Some adoption critics claim less interest in international adoption would mean fewer children in orphanages—and more ethical practices putting them there.

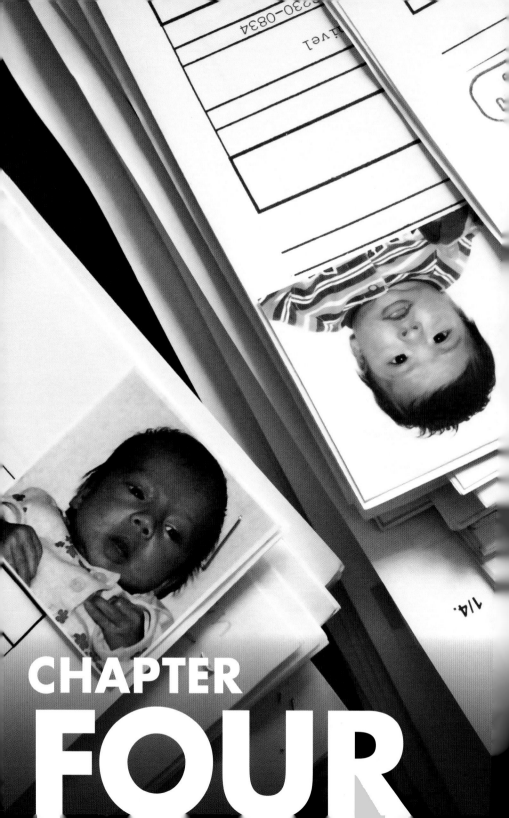

CHAPTER
FOUR

CURBING CORRUPTION

Money is the root of corruption in international adoption systems. The money is not legally exchanged to pay for the adopted children themselves. Rather, it is paid as fees to the people and organizations facilitating the process and sometimes to the biological parents. These fees are always thousands of dollars.[1] In developing nations, this disproportionate amount of money is often worth more to local citizens than it is to the adoptive parent from a wealthy nation paying it. According to the head of American World Adoption, Brian Luwis, the adoption landscape in Ethiopia in recent decades is an example of this, adding, "A lot of people said 'If you give me $5,000, I'll get you a child.'"[2] This leads to "nearly automatic corruption," said Niels Hoogeveen, spokesperson of adoption website Pound Pup Legacy. "Imagine what that sum of money does in a country like Ethiopia, where people make $300 to

Some countries, such as Guatemala, have instituted stricter international adoption protocols to prevent corruption.

$500 a year. All of a sudden, someone received $5,000. That's ten annual incomes. Nearly everyone is corrupt for ten incomes."[3]

Corruption and Kidnapping

Guatemala has experienced similar money-based corruption. "Child finders" there have also paid fees much higher than local wages to find children for agencies. In 2008, the country's total goods and services average per person for the year was $4,700. The fee child finders asked for to find one healthy infant ranged from $6,000 to $8,000.[4] Because this fee was so high, many child finders would simply pay a few thousand dollars of the fee to a poor family for their baby.

In some countries, medical professionals made similar crooked deals. Medical workers in Vietnam were known to coerce impoverished birth mothers with an ultimatum: give up your newborn or pay your expensive hospital bills. Nurses also tricked illiterate mothers into signing documents relinquishing their babies without their knowledge.

During the civil wars in Latin American countries in the 1970s and 1980s, the military internationally trafficked children born to mothers in prisons. Some mothers were already pregnant when imprisoned. Others became pregnant after being raped by their military captors. The children taken from these mothers were placed for adoption with false names and paperwork. According to the military, this was done to avoid the children being raised to become political "subversives" and to keep them from knowing the military had killed, raped, or tortured their parents, which would create a generation that hated the military.

In 2010, reports of kidnappings emerged surrounding the Haitian earthquake. Some were motivated by religion, with kidnappers who wanted to convert the children to their religion. In one case, Laura Silsby, leader of New Life Children's Refuge in

BOOM AND BUST CYCLE OF CORRUPTION

According to Gina Pollock, vice president of Parents for Ethical Adoption Reform, there is a five-step process common in boom-bust adoption situations:
1. A need for adoption is created when there is a large number of children who are in need, usually due to war, poverty, or natural disaster.
2. Many of the children who were originally in need are adopted, but the demand for children from this area has grown.
3. Because there is still a demand but fewer children available for adoption, people begin seeking out children using unethical means to supply the demand.
4. Adoptive parents who suspect they were deceived come forward.
5. Agencies may be shut down or international adoptions from that country halted completely as the boom shifts and begins in another country.[8]

Idaho was caught trying to transport 33 Haitian children out of the country. None of them were orphans. Silsby had no documentation for any of the children and had misled and misinformed their parents. News of the attempted transport was broadcast as "kidnapping for Jesus" in the media.[7] Silsby was arrested and charged with kidnapping and criminal conspiracy, and the children were returned to their parents.

Cases of corruption garner much attention in the news. Certain opponents argue corruption is rampant, citing countries where adoptions are shut down completely due to confirmed cases. Proponents often claim corrupt cases are the minority and a few

In 2014, Chinese authorities successfully shut down a large baby-trafficking ring that offered kidnapped babies for sale over the Internet.

rare cases should not cause the entire system to close. So just how common is corruption in international adoptions? The truth is experts are not sure. As author Gina Kim summed it up in an article in the *Harvard Political Review*, "Because of both faulty bookkeeping and deliberate manipulation, there is no reliable source on how much adoption corruption takes place."[9] With cases of corruption and kidnapping made well known in recent years, some adoptive parents who feel uneasy or suspicious about their child's background hire an adoption searcher. Adoption searchers investigate a child's background, including their adoption paperwork, the status of their family members, and the situations surrounding their adoption, often traveling to the child's hometown for answers. Most adoptive parents want no part in obtaining a child illegally or through corrupt means and are crushed to find out if they unknowingly did so.

"For the most part we try to do everything possible to obscure the fact that international adoption is a market. Adoption agencies paint a pretty picture of children saved and adopted families enriched. Much of this is true. The international adoption business has certainly saved children from poverty, stigmatization, and even death. It has created thousands of hybrid families that are just as happy, sad, and complicated as any other family. But it's still a business, which suffers from all the problems of a business."[10]

—Journalist John Feffer

Weak Governments and New Victims

Many times, governments do not immediately curb corruption because they are simply overwhelmed by the number of adoptions. Additionally, boom periods of adoption often occur in countries that are suffering economically and have governments that lack the finances or power to run effectively. So adoption provides a much-needed revenue source.

When receiving countries realize corruption has become widespread in a country, most begin refusing adoptions from that country. When this happens, as journalist E. J. Graff explained it, "Corruption skips from one unprepared country to . . . another—until that country gets wise, changes its laws, and corrupt adoptions shift to the next unprepared nation."[11]

Legality and Conventions

Corruption and unethical practices are one reason countries and international organizations draft official documents and standards concerning international adoption. There is also a need for international adoption guidelines because it is a process governed by two separate governments—the sending country and the receiving country—that may have different legal principles and policies. Early agreements between countries created between the 1960s and 1980s focused mainly on children's rights and well-being. Corruption was addressed as well, but by the 1980s, as adoptions were increasing around the world, it became clear existing documents could no longer keep up with the new countries becoming involved. In the early 1990s, the Hague Convention, a global agreement, was drafted to provide tools and standards all countries could apply.

The Hague Convention

The Hague Convention on the Protection of Children and Co-operation in Respect of Intercountry Adoption was drafted in 1993. It has become the main instrument governing international adoption and provides a set

CHANGING CONVENTIONS

In 1961, the United Nations Convention on the Reduction of Statelessness was drafted to protect minors' interests and safety in general worldwide. Four years later, the Convention on Jurisdiction, Applicable Law and Recognition of Decrees Relating to Adoptions was drafted, focusing on discussing the power of creating legal decisions and laws that relate to adoption.

In 1986, the United Nations Declaration on Social and Legal Principles Relating to the Protection and Welfare of Children, with Special Reference to Foster Placement and Adoption Nationally and Internationally set several important standards: that international adoption was only to occur when fit parents could not be found in a child's birth country, that children must be deemed legally eligible for adoption, with documentation to prove it, and that "improper financial gain for those involved" in facilitating the adoption process was prohibited.[12]

In 1989, the United Nations Convention on the Rights of the Child stressed the importance of keeping a child's best interests the top priority in all international adoption cases. The convention entered into force in 2007 for the 193 countries that signed and ratified it.[13]

of guidelines and standards that apply to international adoptions around the world.

The major objectives of the Hague Convention are to keep children's welfare as the top consideration and to prevent the sale or trafficking of children. There are four keys to this, according to the convention:

- Using only agencies that have been accredited by proving they use established standards and ethical practices.

- Fully disclosing all fees and money exchanges to ensure they are legitimate.

- Providing children who have been deemed ethically and legally eligible for adoption with special adoption certificates stating so.

- Using updated forms and visas to ensure adoptive parents are eligible to adopt and children are eligible to be adopted.[14]

Responsibilities under the Hague Convention

Sending countries that are a part of the Hague Convention are responsible for making sure a child is

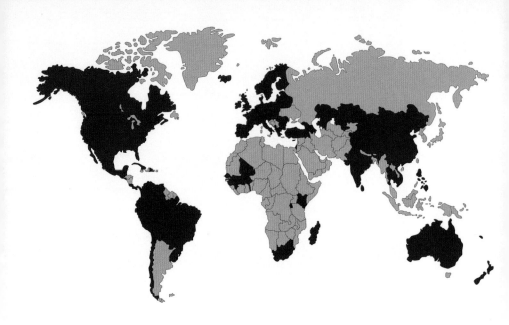

The red countries had ratified the Hague Convention on the Protection of Children and Co-operation in Respect of Intercountry Adoption as of August 2013.

legally eligible to be adopted and that the biological parents are fully consenting and aware of the situation. Receiving countries are to make sure adoptive parents are fit to receive and raise a child.

The Hague Convention entered into force on May 1, 1995. All countries that signed and ratified it are legally responsibly for upholding its standards in international adoptions. Countries may also add to the standards and requirements within their own nation. As of August 2013, 90 countries were a part of the Hague Convention, including the United States.[15] Several other countries had signed it, declaring intention to become a part of the agreement. Countries that are not a part of the convention must still adopt using its guidelines when adopting a child from or sending a child to a Hague Convention country.

The Hague Convention recognizes international adoption as a viable second-best solution to provide children homes and families, after domestic adoption. Domestic adoption is preferred to protect the intangible element of homeland culture and heritage, which cannot be legislated and, once lost, is often impossible to regain.

CHAPTER
FIVE

CULTURE AND RACE

Transcultural adoption is the adoption of a child who is of a different culture than his or her adoptive parents. Adoptions in which children are a different race than the adoptive parents are transracial adoptions. According to the US Department of State, approximately 80 to 85 percent of international adoptions worldwide are transracial.[1] Most are transcultural as well.

Transcultural adoptees typically assimilate to and identify with their adoptive parents' culture, losing their birth culture. According to law professor Jena Martin, some view transcultural adoption as taking members of an undeveloped nation and bringing them to a developed nation, or "modern-day reverse colonization."[2] Transcultural adoption can also cause children to have issues regarding their sense of self and a loss of cultural identity.

Concerns remain that children adopted by parents in foreign countries lose their cultural identities.

57

Forming an Identity

Children begin absorbing culture the moment they are born, through sights, sounds, smells, and tastes. These senses and interactions with caregivers, be they biological parents, nurses, or orphanage staff, also create a sense of culture for infants that continues to grow as they do. When a child is adopted into another culture, all these elements change. Transculturally adopted children immediately begin absorbing the new culture. Rapid assimilation to the new culture occurs because children need to communicate to survive. Critics argue this assimilation is forced or involuntary.

Children begin seeking an understanding of who they are and where they came from early in life. Scholars suggest children

RACE, ETHNICITY, AND CULTURE

Race is something people have no control over. It is their biological heritage, whether they are black, white, Hispanic, or of another race. Ethnicity is a bit more open to interpretation. An ethnic group can be a people grouped together because of racial or religious heritage, or by social tendencies such as language and customs. Race is tied to biology, and ethnicity to culture. An ethnicity can include a country of people, a state, a region, or a neighborhood. Culture is the set of beliefs and ways of life of people of a certain race or ethnicity. It includes language, the way people think, and how they behave and interact in society.

become aware of differences in race around the age of seven.[3] Some report children are aware of physical racial differences at as young as three years old, by four they understand that it places people in different groups, and by five they have developed an attitude toward those groups.[4] Their surrounding culture influences this attitude.

Feeling Different: Where Are You From?

While not always the case, it can be difficult for some transracial foreign adoptees to feel they are truly a part of their new culture when they look different from family members or the majority of people around them. Nicole M. Callahan of the National Council for Adoption states that some adoptees feel talking about feeling and looking differently will only "serve to widen the gap between their experiences and those of their parents."[5]

Many transracial adoptees are often asked, where are you from? This is a question many adopted children think about more deeply later in life, as their sense of self and identity becomes more important to them.

Many transracial adoptees associate more with the race of their adopted family than their own race by the time they are adolescents. This feeling often changes later in life. Many adopted children who recalled wishing they were the race of their adopted culture, or even thinking they were a member of their adoptive race when they were a child, expressed a desire in adulthood to identify with the racial or ethnic heritage of their birth.

Self-Esteem and a Sense of Loss

Many parents have said their younger adopted children do not show a desire or interest in their birth language or culture, so the parents do not discuss it. But according to Dr. Richard Lee of the University of Minnesota, all children who are adopted into another culture experience a sense of loss. He says children who are adopted as infants or when they are very young often do not realize this until later in life, when they become curious about where they are from. Experts say some parents feel it is unnecessary to talk about race with their adopted children—called "color-blind" adoptions—but that they should.[6] Even if the child's race is not an issue to parents, they should discuss race with children before social pressure or others commenting on their race cause the child's self-esteem

Openly discussing race and culture can help adoptive parents alleviate some potential senses of loss for their children later in life.

to suffer. "[My parents] did not talk about my birth heritage nor encourage me to investigate, but rather minimized my ethnicity due to this lack of awareness," said a Korean transracial adoptee named Marijane. "For many years, I downplayed it and tried to fit into the 'whiteness' all around me, never quite feeling like I was good enough, or that I fit into the social norm."[7]

In 2002, an analysis of 93 media reports compiled interviews with transracial adoptees 20 years and older found 82 percent of them had struggled with their ethnic identity at some point in their lives.[8] According to editors of the book *Outsiders from Within: Writing on Transracial Adoption*, "For many transracial adoptees, the pain of loss and unbelonging generated by our living in the borderlands of racial, national, and cultural identities produces a kind of spiritual sickness. It is a malaise that expresses itself in depression, rage, grief, [and] rootlessness."[9]

Reculturation

Some international adoptees have the desire to reconnect with their birth culture. This is called "reculturation." The transcultural adoptee writers who created this term believe all transcultural adoptees seek reculturation at some point in their lives, to different degrees. Some take cultural classes, join groups with members of the same culture, go to cultural summer camps, or take language classes. Homeland tours, where adopted children visit their birth countries to learn about and experience their cultures, are a recent

US Navy officer Michael "Vannak Khem" Misiewicz is reunited with his aunt in Cambodia on his first return trip to his homeland after being adopted as a child.

trend. But reidentifying with birth culture can be just as bumpy a road as fitting into adoptive culture: just as they are labeled as different in their adoptive culture, some adopted children find they are identified as different by their birth culture, too, for having been raised outside it. Additionally, critics of transcultural adoption claim reculturation efforts never really create significant or lasting ties to birth cultures.

Some adopted children seek a more long-term reconnection to their birth country and return there to live. This is called remigration, and it can include taking on a new culturally related name or reclaiming an unused birth name. Moving back to their birth country can be difficult for those adopted at a very young age who have no memories of the culture or surroundings. It can also be complicated if it involves reconnecting with their biological families. Some remigrated adoptees who completely reclaim their birth culture distance themselves from their adoptive families or begin opposing adoptions.

Parental Preparation

Most experts and people who were adopted internationally agree parents must be prepared in order to take on a transracial or transcultural adoptee. They must be ready to help their child make a connection to their birth culture. As Marijane said, "It is the adoptive parents' responsibility to ensure that their child is given opportunities to learn about his or her birth culture beginning at an early age. Otherwise, an injustice is imposed on the children of transracial adoption, whether they are aware of it or not."[10] Parents must also be ready to help the child form an identity in their adoptive culture and address race and the sense of loss children may feel. Nicole Callahan, National Council for Adoption's director of publications, agrees, saying, "When it comes to adoption, and in particular transracial and transcultural adoption, love and good intentions are not enough."[11]

Experts and adoption professionals recognize the negatives of loss of culture are significant. But many argue international adoption helps prevent the loss of something more serious than loss of culture: the loss of human rights.

PREPARING PARENTS

Pamela Severs of the North American Resource Center for Child Welfare wrote in the book *Growing Up Adopted* an extensive list of questions and considerations parents should ask themselves before adopting a child of another culture and race. According to Severs, parents should recognize what they know of other cultures. They should consider the support they and the adopted child will receive from neighbors, family members, friends, and other people around them. They should also consider the cultural and racial diversity in their communities, schools, and social circles and whether the child will have role models or people to relate to of their race or culture. Article 30 of the United Nations Convention on the Rights of the Child states all children have the right to develop connections to people from the same origins: "In those States in which ethnic, religious or linguistic minorities or persons of indigenous origin exist, a child belonging to such a minority or who is indigenous shall not be denied the right . . . to enjoy his or her own culture."[12]

CHAPTER
SIX

INSTITUTIONS, HUMAN RIGHTS, AND HEALTH

R omania's worst orphanages in the 1990s received major media attention. Stories depicted children being neglected, living on top of one another in run-down buildings. Children with physical and mental disabilities were dirty and suffering. Nearly all the children were malnourished, and some were chained to beds while others were lying on bare cement. Studies of orphanages in China during the same decade returned similarly shocking depictions. In certain orphanages, some children were neglected to the point of death. Some starved or were left in rooms to die alone.

Not all—or even most—orphanages are the dirty, grim, overcrowded places depicted in the documentaries of the 1990s. And many that used to have poor conditions have improved. But experts say

Living in orphanages and institutions can have lasting effects on children, who often do not receive enough care and attention.

nothing can replace or compare to the love and attention a child receives in a home. Living in an institution for a significant amount of time has been proven to cause physical, social, emotional, and mental delays and disorders that last for life. Many experts argue the issues of corruption, trafficking, and loss of culture dim when compared to effects of institutionalization.

Institutions

There is often a shortage of caregivers in orphanages, so children receive less one-on-one interaction. In countries that struggle economically, orphanages may have few or no toys, not enough or poor quality food, a bleak atmosphere with few windows, or not enough room for children to have their own space.

When children spend significant time—often cited as six months or longer—in an institution, they can become institutionalized, which causes delayed mental and physical growth and the development of physical, social, and mental disorders. Effects worsen the longer children live in an institution.

Children living in institutions may be physically smaller than other children their age. Some struggle with physical functions such as motor skills. Sensory integration, or the processing of senses, such as touch, taste, smell, sight, and hearing, can also become atypical or troubled.

Other physical problems of living in an institution can include a higher probability of having crossed eyes, which may be due to an infant's lack of objects to focus on when they are developing. Children in institutions are also more likely to catch infectious diseases.

Research from a years-long study of 136 Romanian children who lived in orphanages when they were young found institutionalization changes a child's brain function and structure.[1] Neglect can lead to a multitude of mental disorders and delays, as well as social and language disorders.

SENSORY PROBLEMS

In 2005, 60 children adopted from Eastern Europe were given tests and questionnaires to determine their sensory integration. The children were between four and almost nine years old. Half of the group had been institutionalized for a mean time of two years and ten months. The other half had been institutionalized for less time, a mean of three months. The results were that the group that had been institutionalized for longer scored lower on sensory integration. The study determined this occurred because children in institutions are often deprived of exposure to sensory and environmental exploration during early childhood.[2]

NEGLECT AND MENTAL DISORDERS

Neglect can cause children to show symptoms similar to autism, a disorder that affects social behavior and spoken or physical communication. Trouble with language or social behavior in general is common in institutionalized children. Experts have reported institutionalized children adopted from abroad have higher probability of schizophrenia, bipolar disease, and attention deficit hyperactivity disorder (ADHD), among other mental disorders.

Odd behavior and behavioral problems are also effects of institutionalization. Some children hide food in their pockets, bedrooms, or cheeks, an effect of not having enough food in an orphanage. Some children are overly affectionate to everyone, even strangers. This is because they want attention so badly and are used to fighting for it with other children when a stranger visits the orphanage. Once adopted, some institutionalized children hardly let new parents out of their sight, afraid to be abandoned. Some children act out angrily to push their adoptive family to the limits as a test to see if they truly want the child enough to put up with such behavior. Children may also develop reactive attachment disorder, which makes it hard for them to attach to adoptive parents and accept love. This is most common in internationally adopted children who were neglected or abused while living in an orphanage.

The AIDS epidemic has left many orphaned children in Kenya, who are sent to orphanages. Some of these children escape institutionalization by being adopted internationally.

Institutionalization can affect adoptees past childhood, causing them to be unprepared for living a healthy emotional life as an adult. Many experts involved in the international adoption debate feel the severe and lasting effects of institutionalization should trump any rights to culture and override concerns about corruption that can keep children from being placed in homes.

Children's Rights v. Culture Loss and Corruption

Corruption and controversy over issues such as loss of culture, trafficking, and coercion of birth parents have led some countries to develop stricter regulations for international adoption. This leads to more children left in institutions for longer—possibly even until they reach adulthood, or for life if they have severe disabilities.

Many international adoption advocates agree the physical and mental damage caused by institutionalization is a violation of a child's basic human rights, and that these effects are more serious than loss of culture. As international law professor Sara Dillon states, "In no sense could the right of a child to enjoy a particular culture be said to trump the more fundamental right to be loved and protected as an individual."[3] Journalist Chuck Johnson reasoned, "How much can a child living in an orphanage truly benefit from her culture, if her most basic daily needs—as

WHAT ABOUT FOSTER HOMES?

Another option for children in need of homes is foster care, also called interim care, a government system in which children are placed in a designated home for temporary care while awaiting adoption, rather than staying in an orphanage. But critics of foster care say that although it is possibly a better alternative to an orphanage, it does not provide permanent connections and stability, so it is not a good long-term solution either. Children living in foster homes do not suffer from institutionalization, but they do have other issues, such as the fear of abandonment and lack stable attachments. Group homes in which small groups of people live together are another alternative. But many agree that while group homes and foster homes are better than institutions, they are still not as good as an adoptive family. They still do not foster stable attachments, so children can have psychological troubles from living there.

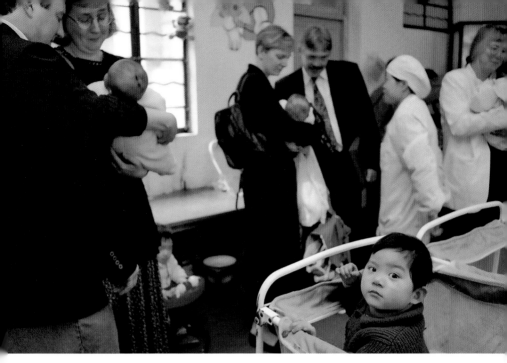

The one-on-one attention and care offered by a loving home and adoptive parents gives children a lesser risk of suffering the effects of life in an institution.

well as her long-term health and well-being—are not guaranteed?"[4]

Corruption is another issue children's rights advocates argue makes institutionalization worse. When corruption erupts, the adoption system begins adopting out the children a receiving country wants, not the ones who truly need families: those who are sick, troubled, or have some sort of disability. These children remain in orphanages, where institutionalization sets in or worsens. In recent years, maltreatment that occurs after children are adopted has become another pressing problem.

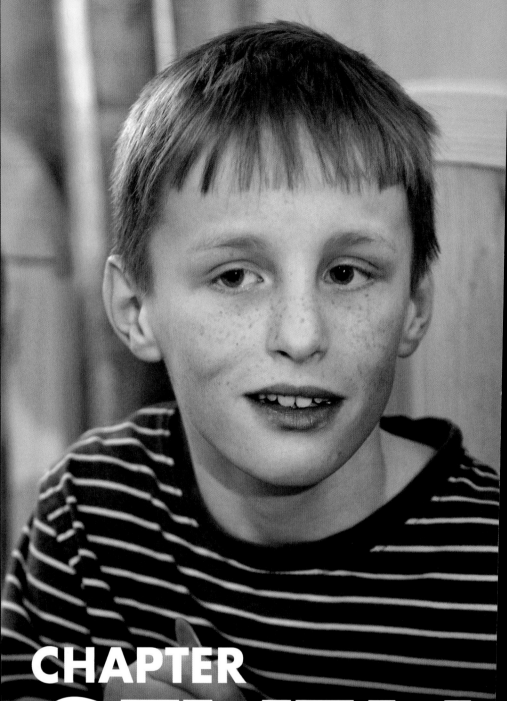

CHAPTER
SEVEN

RE-HOMING AND ABUSE

O n April 7, 2010, a boy stepped from a plane into a bustling airport. The seven-year-old arrived in Russia alone. He had been alone on the 11-hour flight that brought him there from the United States. Artyom had had two mothers and lived on two continents in his short life. His adoptive mother, Torry Ann, had welcomed Artyom into her Tennessee home just six months before. She renamed him Justin. Their relationship quickly became strained as Justin acted out. Torry Ann grew frustrated and, she claims, scared of her adoptive son. She decided to send Justin back to Russia, as though he were a package that could be returned. Justin reentered his birth country carrying a backpack with a note from Torry Ann tucked inside. "I no longer wish to parent this child," it read. "He is violent and has severe psychopathic issues."[1]

Seven-year-old Artyom's adoptive mother sent him back to Moscow, Russia, alone with a note, some cookies, and crayons.

75

ARTYOM/JUSTIN

Artyom's biological mother cared for him until he was six years old, when he was taken from her due to her alcoholism. From there, Artyom spent time in a "grim orphanage" before being adopted by Tennessean Torry Ann when he was seven years old in 2009. Being taken from his mother was undoubtedly hard for Artyom. As US psychotherapist Joe Soll explained, "When you remove a child from a family, no matter what the circumstances are, it's a trauma."[3] Torry Ann spent four days with Artyom, whom she renamed Justin, before adopting him. During the six months he lived with Tory Ann, she claims Justin created a "hit list" of people to kill and threatened to burn down the house. She shipped him back to Russia, becoming the target of worldwide scorn and disgust. As of 2012, Artyom lived in a group home in Moscow and said he "tries to forget" about his time living in the United States.[4]

News of the situation spread throughout the United States and Russia. Both nations were horrified that a child was "shipped home like a faulty product," as Torry Ann's neighbors put it.[2] International adoptions from Russia to the United States were halted. Artyom's situation was an extreme example of a phenomenon that has become somewhat common in recent years: parents who wish to stop caring for adopted children, sending them back or finding them a different home.

Re-homing

When an adoptive parent finds an adopted child a new home, it is called "re-homing." Parents re-home children because they feel overwhelmed or believe the children are not adjusting in their homes. As of the fall of 2013, nearly all cases of re-homed children living in the United States were children who were initially adopted from abroad. This is partly due to the shifting profile of children available for international adoption today. According to Dr. Elaine Schulte, the medical director of the International Adoption Program at the Cleveland Clinic Children's Hospital, in 2010, 80 percent of international adoptees had special needs or developmental issues.[5]

Some parents who have re-homed children were aware of the child's disorders or problems before adopting them, but thought they could handle them. Others did not have information on their child's medical background and were surprised when disorders or issues were revealed. Some have claimed adoption agencies abroad purposefully hid a child's sicknesses or disorders from them. As Adam Pertman explained,

> [The occurrences of re-homing] should be understood as a cautionary tale about what can happen when parents are not prepared for the needs of the children they adopt, and don't receive the necessary training, support, or services to meet those needs. It also should be seen as the tip of an iceberg of unmonitored, unregulated adoption-related activities taking place on the Internet.[6]

Another reason more international children are re-homed in the United States is because children adopted domestically have the foster care system to fall back on in extreme situations. When a parent wants to stop caring for an internationally adopted child, it is more difficult to legally provide the child a new home or return the child to their birth country. An investigation is likely to follow, and adoptive parents might have to pay additional costs to support the child in their home country as other arrangements are made. So some parents take an easier, cheaper route and find new parents themselves, outside the legal system.

How Are Families for Re-homing Found?

New York Times columnist Nicholas Kristof said re-homing occurs with "less formality than the transfer of a car."[7] Others have compared the entire process to people finding new homes for their pets. Parents turn to Internet forums and chat groups to post ads for their children and seek new homes. There are no home studies, background checks, or legal authorities involved. It is often as simple as chatting with an interested parent and setting up a time and place to meet for the transfer. The entire process can happen in days or weeks. In the fall of 2013, the news organization Reuters released a five-part report on its investigative look into re-homing. It found that on a certain online forum, which has since been shut down, there was an average of one child being re-homed each week. One adopted girl from Russia was placed in three different homes within six months.[8] Sometimes the same forum participants would post ads giving up children while putting out queries seeking other children.

Legality and New Families' Motivations

With international adoptions, there are many legal steps taken to finalize an adoption. How can care be transferred so simply by finding new parents online? Adoptive families give the new

RE-HOMING FORUM LISTINGS

In Reuters' investigation of re-homing, the news organization examined five years of online forums. The report found the youngest child advertised was ten months old, and the majority were six to 14 years old. Most were adopted internationally. Below is a sampling of actual ads listed on forums, as reported by Reuters:

"Born in October of 2000—this handsome boy, 'Rick' was placed from India a year ago and is obedient and eager to please."

"I am totally ashamed to say it but we do truly hate this boy!"

"We adopted an 8-year-old girl from China. . . . Unfortunately, we are now struggling having been home for 5 days."[9]

Re-homing not only takes a psychological toll on children but can put them in dangerous situations with adults with bad intentions.

families power of attorney when re-homing. This is a document that states they are to be the new guardians of the child. The document does not transfer complete custody, but does allow guardians to house a child, enroll him or her in school, and collect government incentives, such as tax deductions, for raising the child. Power of attorney granting guardianship is intended for financial or legal situations in which a child needs to live with extended family members. But re-homing has exploited these allowances, leading many people to re-home children without attracting the suspicion of child welfare and protective services.

Why do parents who take in re-homed children want to do so in the first place? Gaining a child through re-homing is a cheap or free way to adopt a child. It is also a way to adopt a child while avoiding increasing restrictions on international adoptions. As one online forum member said, re-homing is "the 'latest country' to adopt from."[10]

Some children become victims of abuse and neglect in their new homes. Some are given to parents who have already had their biological children or other adoptive children taken away, such as US mother Nicole Eason, who was featured in Reuters' investigative reports. A mother of two, Eason had lost custody of her biological children and had been accused of sexual abuse by children she babysat. Despite this history, Eason took in a total of six children through re-homing.

Abuse

Because re-homing bypasses home studies and adoptive parent requirements, the process can attract parents with impure intent—people such as pedophiles and abusers. Some communities see a pattern of large Christian fundamentalist families adopting many children in order to convert them, but ending up abusing or re-homing them instead.

In 2011, an Ethiopian girl died in Washington. She was found outside, without clothes, in the cold rain. Hana had been adopted in 2009, and since then she and another Ethiopian adoptee had been made to sleep in a closet, shower in the yard under a hose, and eat outside even in rain and snow. Her adoptive parents' biological children suffered no such abuses. Hana's adoptive parents were Christian fundamentalists. Their religion encouraged them to have a large family, and

THE EASONS

In 2008, Nicole Eason and her husband, Calvin, responded to an online ad seeking a new home for an adopted girl from Liberia. Quita was 16 years old and had been adopted by Todd and Melissa in Washington. The couple had raised Quita for two years and said she had significant behavioral and health problems. Nicole and Calvin said they could handle it. One week after chatting online, the four met and made the exchange. Days later, when Todd and Melissa tried to call and check up on Quita, they learned she had never been to school. Police found their home vacant. Police reports also revealed Nicole's past: her two biological children had been taken from her, she had been accused of sexual abuse, and she had been described by one officer as having "severe psychiatric problems as well with violent tendencies."[11] Police found Nicole, Calvin, and Quita in New York, at Nicole's mother's home. Quita was returned to the adoptive parents who had discarded her just weeks before. Authorities did not press charges on either set of parents.

After the incident, Reuters interviewed Nicole outside an Arizona hotel, where she and her husband were living at the time. When asked if she was considering taking on more re-homed children, Nicole said, "Yes. I have kids in my room."[12]

they believed in strict rules as the way to save their adopted children's souls. They were also followers of a controversial book that promoted child control and abuse, which was popular with other families of the same convictions.

In the 1990s, 15 Russian adoptees were murdered by their US adoptive parents.[13] Several more were abused. As of February 2013, it was cited that of the 60,000 Russian children who had been adopted into the United States in the past 20 years, a total of 19 had died.[14] The reported death of a three-year-old Russian adoptee in Texas in January 2013, which was ruled as accidental rather than stemming from abuse, infuriated Russian officials and citizens. That month, a law went into effect banning US adoptions of Russian children. The bill was named after one of the deceased Russian children. One year after Russia enacted the US ban on adopting internationally, it was reported by a Russian source that a total of 259 pending adoptions into the United States had been stopped.[15]

Issues of abuse and murder have infuriated some sending countries, and, as in Russia's case, caused them to reduce or close off international adoptions. This in turn has raised fears of children becoming institutionalized because they can no longer be adopted internationally. Between institutionalization, re-homing, abuse, corruption, trafficking, and loss of culture, a variety of solutions will be necessary to improve today's international adoption system.

SUGGESTED MEDICAL TESTING

When adopted children leave their birth country before officially entering the United States, they undergo a medical examination. According to professor of pediatrics and medicine Myron Levin at the University of Colorado-Denver, in "more than 50 percent of cases a significant medical diagnosis is missed by the US Immigration and Naturalization Service–approved exit examination."[16] Experts and doctors suggest adoptive parents take their children to a follow-up examination in the United States as well, within a couple weeks of arriving. During the examination, doctors suggest a full check of the child's physical, mental, and emotional health, so parents can become better prepared and informed to raise the child. However, a number of diseases or disorders don't manifest until children are older.

In 2013, demonstrators in Moscow rally in support of a US adoption ban after news of the deaths of Russian adopted children spread.

CHAPTER
EIGHT

INTERNATIONAL ADOPTION TODAY

International adoption has decreased globally in recent years. Numbers in the United States reflect this: in 2004, there were 23,000 international adoptions made in the United States.[1] In 2012, there were fewer than 9,000.[2] This decline developed because of practice and policy changes in international adoption. The decline means more children are at risk of becoming institutionalized, or dying because of poverty and war. And corruption, abuse, re-homing, and cultural loss are still issues. Several scholars and organizations are seeking solutions for international adoption today.

In 2013, the Donaldson Adoption Institute released *A Changing World: Shaping Best Practices through Understanding of the New Realities of Intercountry Adoption*. The report describes itself as "the most extensive independent research into intercountry adoption to date."[3] It examines how international adoption has changed and

Thousands of international adopted children are placed in loving homes in the United States every year.

what system alterations are needed today to address ongoing issues. Other adoption experts have also suggested solutions to address issues and better regulate the system.

Changing Profiles and Preventing Institutionalization

Today, the demographic of internationally adopted children has changed. Many children up for adoption are older and have special needs. Some sending countries have begun allowing or promoting only international adoption of these children. The president of the National Council for Adoption, Chuck Johnson, believes children are "getting older and that probably means they've been in the institutional system longer, which will increase their chances of [having] special needs."[4]

To stop corruption and adoptee abuse, sending countries have developed stricter regulations. However, these cause children to spend longer amounts of time in institutions. Adoption agencies have called to improve and reshape international adoption laws to reflect the current demographic of older or special needs children stuck in institutions.

Some couples choose to adopt children with disabilities, hoping to provide a better future for these children who might not otherwise be adopted.

The Donaldson report suggests children in institutions should be assessed regularly to ensure they are not developing disorders or delays. Keeping children healthy will increase their chance of being adopted either domestically or internationally. The study also suggests speeding up the process of deciding whether a child can live with extended family or be adopted domestically, or whether the child should become eligible for international adoption. This would decrease the time the child lives in an institution.

Author Kathryn Joyce states, "Part of the reason adoption is so inadequately regulated is that adoption agencies, through their representative trade groups and advocacy organizations, have had a heavy hand in crafting the laws and institutions that govern their own behavior."[7] In other words, agencies have a large part in helping create the laws and rules by which they have to abide. Maureen Flatley, an advocate for child welfare, agrees: "We're not turning to oil companies to draft the safety regulations, but in adoption and child welfare it's always the industry that gets called on. So there's no oversight, no accountability, no real penalties for anything."[8]

Sara Dillon agrees, and said a "global agency" is needed to examine where the children are living and what situation would be the best option for them, and then act quickly. The hope is that minimizing the number of institutionalized children will both protect human rights and reduce instances of re-homing.

Solutions for Re-homing and Corruption

The Donaldson study found that although fewer than 25 percent of parents interviewed expected to adopt children with special needs, 47 percent actually did.[5] Even when special needs are not involved, "Adoption is known to make psychological demands on the parties beyond those of natural parenthood," according to Masson.[6] For this reason, she suggests there be adequate research and knowledge of a child's situation and that the complete situation be relayed to parents before the adoption takes place. Parents who adopt children with special needs should be educated and offered resources to help them adjust. Sending and receiving countries can do their part to prevent re-homing by providing adoptive families continuous support as they raise a child.

When it comes to addressing corruption, thus far, the only answer has been to shut down international adoptions to or from a particular country. This is not a solution for many experts and advocates. As Pertman said, "Ensuring that all the other kids that need loving homes don't get them is not the way to solve the problem."[9] Experts suggest more time and attention be paid to each case of international adoption to prevent adoptions facilitated unethically.

However, Dillon admits that taking more time to investigate each child is not an easy task when experts are also calling for quicker decision making to keep children out of institutions. To do damage control for cases where a child becomes adopted through unethical means, the Donaldson report suggests a global policy be implemented to correct the adoption and return the child to his or her parents.

Managing Money

Many believe the solution to solving corrupt practices in international adoptions lies in reassessing the money involved in the process. As journalist Graff suggests,

> More effective regulations would strictly limit the amount of money that changes hands. Per-child fees could be outlawed. Payments could be capped to cover only legitimate costs such as medical care, food, and clothing for the children. And crucially, fees must be kept proportionate with the local economies.[10]

Thomas DiFilippo, the president of the Joint Council on International Children's Services, agreed, "If we have the greatest laws and the greatest regulations but are still sending $20,000 cash . . . you can bypass the system with enough cash."[11]

There has also been progress in enacting laws to make profiting from improper international adoptions criminal. Brazil and Germany made it criminal to traffic children. Any Romanian parties involved in adoption who accept extra money can go to prison.

Retaining Contact

Another suggestion for curbing corruption is to have international adoptees retain contact with their biological families through open adoptions. In addition to ensuring biological parents aren't misled into giving up their child, this will also allow a child to keep some connection to his or her birth culture and form a cultural identity.

The Donaldson report found that many parents today—approximately 35 percent—still choose international adoption to avoid contact with biological families.[12] However, it also revealed many change their minds and seek to help their adopted child reconnect with their birth family and culture. Open international adoptions have increased. However, it remains difficult for poor families with limited resources to retain contact.

"Many who oppose intercountry adoption offer no viable alternative for orphaned, abandoned, and vulnerable children, other than a continuation of the status quo. While ethnic, cultural, and national identity are all important, children also need love, security, nurturing, education, and purpose—all of which is best provided by a permanent, loving family. . . . Tragically, the decline in intercountry adoption means that too many of these children will never realize their intrinsic right to a family. . . . Intercountry adoption must remain an important part of a complete, holistic child welfare policy."[13]
—William Rosen, chair of National Council for Adoption International Committee

The Future of International Adoption

The processes of international adoption today have more transparency and are more consistent. Although governance is different from country to country, overall, there is a general increase in keeping children's best interests in focus.

International adoption practices change quickly, and making sure policies support the realties of international

CELEBRITY CONTROVERSY

In 2002, American actress Angelina Jolie adopted a son from Cambodia. In the next several years, she adopted two more children with the support of her partner, Brad Pitt: a daughter from Ethiopia and a son from Vietnam. After Jolie adopted her daughter in 2005, the media uncovered a lie told about the girl's biological mother. Jolie had been told the girl's mother died. In truth, her mother wanted to keep and raise her but lived in poverty. She put her up for adoption rather than watch her suffer from malnutrition. Jolie had received wide praise for her international adoption of the girl. One and one-half years later, Jolie spoke out publicly when American singer Madonna adopted a son from Malawi. Jolie stated Malawi did not have a legal system intact to process adoptions and that Madonna knew it. Madonna was the target of criticism from the press as well. Much of the controversy came from the fact that the boy's father was still alive, and he had had to give up his son for adoption due to poverty. Some argued Jolie's situation was no different. In addition, unsettling details regarding Jolie's first adoption surfaced. The agency Jolie used was accused of fraud, corruption, and child stealing. International adoptions from the country were stopped. Despite ongoing controversies, celebrities continue to adopt internationally.

Angelina Jolie has internationally adopted children from Cambodia, Ethiopia, and Vietnam.

adoption remains a challenge. Abolitionists continue arguing for the complete end to international adoption, as promoters work to prove this is a violation of a child's right to a family. Perhaps the third side best characterizes the future of international adoption: pragmatists know international adoption is a practice that will continue and so work to increase knowledge, strengthen policies, and improve regulations. Those on all sides of international adoption have in common the desire to protect children's futures and, as the Donaldson report explains, "enhance their prospects for better lives."[14]

TIMELINE

Late 1940s
The first major wave of international adoptions follows the end of World War II, rescuing war orphans.

1948–1969
More than 50,000 children are adopted internationally.

1950s–1960s
A second major wave of international adoptions follows the Korean War.

1954
Harry and Bertha Holt see a documentary about Korean orphans and are inspired to adopt eight of them.

1956
The Holts establish Holt International Children's Services, which becomes the largest and longest-running US adoption agency.

1961

The United Nations Convention on the Reduction of Statelessness is drafted with a main goal of protecting minors' interests worldwide.

1965

The Convention on Jurisdiction, Applicable Law and Recognition of Decrees Relating to Adoptions is drafted to discuss creating laws that relate to adoption.

1970s–1980s

Corruption in Latin America leads to the military engaging in kidnappings and unethical adoptions.

Late 1970s

War orphans are airlifted out of Vietnam and adopted abroad.

1980

China implements its one-child policy nationwide.

1986

The United Nations Declaration on Social and Legal Principles Relating to the Protection and Welfare of Children, with Special Reference to Foster Placement and Adoption Nationally and Internationally is created, introducing several international adoption guidelines.

TIMELINE

1989

The United Nations Convention on the Rights of the Child is created and stresses giving children's best interests top consideration in international adoptions.

1990s

Footage of grim, overcrowded Romanian orphanages is broadcast and many international adoptions from the country follow.

1990s

Fifteen international adoptees from Russia are murdered by their adoptive parents and many others are abused.

1993

The Hague Convention on the Protection of Children and Co-operation in Respect of Intercountry Adoption is created.

1995

On May 1, the Hague Convention becomes the main legal instrument guiding international adoption.

1990s–2000s
AIDS epidemics in African countries lead to many international adoptions leaving the region.

2000s
Natural disasters such as the tsunami in the Indian Ocean in 2004 and the earthquake in Haiti in 2010 lead to large movements of international adoption out of these areas.

2007
The United Nations Convention on the Rights of the Child enters into force.

2010
Seven-year-old Artyom is sent back to Russia by his adoptive US mother on April 7.

2011
Hana from Ethiopia dies at her adoptive parents' home in Washington after suffering two years of abuse.

2013
In October, the Donaldson Adoption Institute releases a thorough report on the international adoption landscape today and suggests solutions for issues.

ESSENTIAL FACTS

At Issue

- International adoption is the adoption of children from one country into another. It is controversial for several reasons, and creates debate both for and against its practice.

- Negative issues surrounding international adoption include children losing their connection with their birth culture and high adoption fees creating corruption within adoption systems.

- Trafficking has become a major concern surrounding international adoptions; many children are kidnapped or bought or coerced from parents for a price.

- Positive effects of international adoption include providing children who have little or no chance of being adopted domestically a chance to have a family, removing children from areas of conflict or disaster, and preventing institutionalization.

- The threat of institutionalization is increasing with the decline of international adoptions and stricter regulations.

- Re-homing, when adoptive parents no longer wish to parent an adopted child and find them a new home, has increased.

- International adoptions are declining worldwide, which exacerbates the problems of institutionalization and does not seem to be completely stamping out other issues.

Critical Dates

1945

The end of World War II created the first instance of large-scale international adoption as people desired to rescue children orphaned by the war.

1954

The Holts' adoption of Korean children following the Korean War influenced the future of international adoption.

1993

The drafting of the Hague Convention on the Protection of Children and Co-operation in Respect of Intercountry Adoption created worldwide guidelines and standards for ethical adoption practices.

Quote

"The emotional nature of intercountry adoption often leads each side to demonize the other, impeding the ability to find common ground. Moreover, keeping the debate focused on whether intercountry adoption is good or bad is problematic; there will always be compelling arguments on either side, and compelling reasons to which each can point in support of their position. As such, focusing on the positives or negatives in the debate amounts to a stand-off in which neither side is willing to compromise any ground, a perpetual lose-lose situation."—*Jena Martin, author of* The Good, The Bad, and The Ugly: The New Way of Looking at the Intercountry Adoption Debate

GLOSSARY

assimilation
The process of getting used to and becoming part of a new culture or country.

communism
An economic system based on the elimination of private ownership of factories, land, and other means of economic production.

evangelization
The spreading of the teachings of Christianity.

fascism
A system based on a government ruled by a dictator who makes all decisions for the country's people.

institutionalization
The mental, physical, and social effects of living in an institution for an extended period of time.

institutionalized
To be put in an institution.

motor skill
A learned movement that makes everyday actions easy and natural.

open adoption

An adoption made directly between a biological parent and adoptive parents, with the help of a facilitator in cases of international adoption.

pedophile

A person who is sexually attracted to children.

protocol

Rules that govern how to act or what steps to formally take.

sterilization

When a person is made unable to have children through some type of procedure.

visa

An official document stating a person can enter, leave, or live in a country for a certain amount of time.

ADDITIONAL RESOURCES

Selected Bibliography

Bartholet, Elizabeth. *Nobody's Children: Abuse and Neglect, Foster Drift, and the Adoption Alternative*. Boston: Beacon, 2000. Print.

Briggs, Laura. *Somebody's Children: The Politics of Transracial and Transnational Adoption*. Durham, NC: Duke UP, 2013. Print.

Mabry, Cynthia, and Lisa Kelly. *Adoption Law: Theory, Policy, and Practice*. Getsville, NY: William S. Hein, 2010. Print.

Further Readings

Bowen, Richard. *Mei Mei—Little Sister: Portraits from a Chinese Orphanage*. San Francisco: Chronicle, 2005. Print.

Haerens, Margaret. *International Adoption*. Detroit, MI: Greenhaven, 2011. Print.

Warren, Andrea. *Escape from Saigon: How a Vietnam War Orphan Became an American Boy*. New York: Square Fish-Macmillan, 2004. Print.

Websites

To learn more about Essential Issues, visit **booklinks.abdopublishing.com**. These links are routinely monitored and updated to provide the most current information available.

For More Information

For more information on this subject, contact or visit the following organizations:

Intercountry Adoption
Bureau of Consular Affairs, US Department of State
Office of Children's Issues
CA/OCS/CI   SA-17, 9th Floor
Washington, DC 20522-1709
1-888-407-4747
http://adoption.state.gov
The US Department of State provides guidance for US parents interested in international adoption and anyone wanting to learn more about policies and processes.

National Council for Adoption
225 N. Washington Street
Alexandria, VA 22314-2561
703-299-6633
https://www.adoptioncouncil.org
A national advocacy organization, the NCFA's website provides several useful links for research of international adoption.

SOURCE NOTES

Chapter 1. In Need of a Home

1. Kevin Voigt and Sophie Brown. "International Adoptions in Decline as Number of Orphans Grows." *CNN: World*. Cable News Network, 15 Oct. 2008. Web. 17 Sept. 2013.

2. "What Is Human Trafficking?" *Stop the Traffik*. Stop the Traffik, 2013. Web. 8 Dec. 2013.

3. Jena Martin. "The Good, The Bad, and The Ugly: The New Way of Looking at the Intercountry Adoption Debate (pdf)." *UC Davis Journal of International Law and Policy*. Regents of the University of California, 14 May 2007. Web. 12 Dec. 2013. 174.

4. Judith Masson. "Intercountry Adoption: A Global Problem or a Global Solution?" *Journal of International Affairs* 55.1 (Fall 2001): 148. *EBSCO Host*. Web. 12 Dec. 2013.

Chapter 2. History of International Adoption

1. Peter Selman. "Global Trends in Intercountry Adoption: 2001–2010." *Adoption Advocate* 44 (Feb. 2012): 4. *Expanded Academic ASAP (Gale)*. Web. 10 Dec. 2013.

2. Ibid. 1–2.

3. Kathryn Joyce. *The Child Catchers: Rescue, Trafficking, and the New Gospel of Adoption*. Jackson, TN: PublicAffairs-Perseus, 2013. Print. 49.

4. Peter Selman. "Global Trends in Intercountry Adoption: 2001–2010." *Adoption Advocate* 44 (Feb. 2012): 4. *Expanded Academic ASAP (Gale)*. Web. 10 Dec. 2013.

5. Laura Briggs. *Somebody's Children: The Politics of Transracial and Transnational Adoption*. Durham, NC: Duke UP, 2013. Print. 156.

6. Saralee Kane. "The Movement of Children for International Adoption: An Epidemiologic Perspective." *Social Science Journal* 30.4 (1993). *EBSCO Host*. Web. 8 Dec. 2013.

7. "One-Child Policy." *Encyclopædia Britannica*. Encyclopædia Britannica, 2013. Web. 12 Dec. 2013.

8. Peter Selman. "Global Trends in Intercountry Adoption: 2001–2010." *Adoption Advocate* 44 (Feb. 2012): 5. *Expanded Academic ASAP (Gale)*. Web. 10 Dec. 2013.

9. Ibid. 9.

10. Kathryn Joyce. *The Child Catchers: Rescue, Trafficking, and the New Gospel of Adoption*. Jackson, TN: PublicAffairs-Perseus, 2013. Print. 5.

Chapter 3. Adopters and Adoptees

1. "Child Adoption: Trends and Policies (pdf)." *United Nations*. United Nations Department of Economic and Social Affairs Population Division, 2009. Web. 11 Dec. 2013. xviii.

2. Ibid. 65.

3. "Child Adoption: Trends and Policies (pdf)." *United Nations*. United Nations Department of Economic and Social Affairs Population Division, 2009. Web. 11 Dec. 2013. 91.

4. "Statistics." *Intercountry Adoption*. Bureau of Consular Affairs, US Department of State, n.d. Web. 13 Dec. 2013.

5. Sharon Jayson. "International Adoptions: Kids Older, Have Special Needs." *USA TODAY*. Today/Gannett, 30 Oct. 2013. Web. 13 Dec. 2013.

6. Ellen Pinderhughes, et al. "A Changing World: Shaping Best Practices through Understanding of the New Realities of Intercountry Adoption." *Evan B. Donaldson Adoption Institute*. Donaldson Adoption Institute, Oct. 2013. Web. 15 Dec. 2013.

7. E. J. Graff. "The Lie We Love." *Foreign Policy*. Foreign Policy, 10 Sep. 2010. Web. 12 Dec. 2013.

8. Cynthia R. Howard and Chandy C. John. "International Adoption." *Centers for Disease Control and Prevention*. CDC, n.d. Web. 14 Dec. 2013.

9. Kathryn Joyce. *The Child Catchers: Rescue, Trafficking, and the New Gospel of Adoption*. Jackson, TN: PublicAffairs-Perseus, 2013. Print. 155.

Chapter 4. Curbing Corruption

1. Gina Kim. "International Adoption's Trafficking Problem." *Harvard Political Review*. Harvard Political Review, 20 June 2012. Web. 10 Nov. 2013.

2. Kathryn Joyce. *The Child Catchers: Rescue, Trafficking, and the New Gospel of Adoption*. Jackson, TN: PublicAffairs-Perseus, 2013. Print. 136.

3. Ibid.

4. E. J. Graff. "The Lie We Love." *Foreign Policy*. Foreign Policy, 10 Sept. 2010. Web. 12 Dec. 2013.

5. Kathryn Joyce. *The Child Catchers: Rescue, Trafficking, and the New Gospel of Adoption*. Jackson, TN: PublicAffairs-Perseus, 2013. Print. 132.

6. E. J. Graff. "The Lie We Love." *Foreign Policy*. Foreign Policy, 10 Sept. 2010. Web. 12 Dec. 2013.

7. Kathryn Joyce. *The Child Catchers: Rescue, Trafficking, and the New Gospel of Adoption*. Jackson, TN: PublicAffairs-Perseus, 2013. Print. 6.

8. Ibid. 171.

9. Gina Kim. "International Adoption's Trafficking Problem." *Harvard Political Review*. Harvard Political Review, 20 June 2012. Web. 10 Nov. 2013.

10. John Feffer. "The Baby Trade." *Foreign Policy in Focus*. Foreign Policy in Focus, 22 Dec. 2010. Web. 13 Dec. 2013.

11. Kathryn Joyce. *The Child Catchers: Rescue, Trafficking, and the New Gospel of Adoption*. Jackson, TN: PublicAffairs-Perseus, 2013. Print. 132.

12. "Child Adoption: Trends and Policies (pdf)." *United Nations*. United Nations Department of Economic and Social Affairs Population Division, 2009. Web. 11 Dec. 2013. 54.

13. Ibid.

14. "Understanding the Hague Convention." *Intercountry Adoption*. Bureau of Consular Affairs, US Department of State, n.d. Web. 12 Dec. 2013.

15. "Convention Countries." *Intercountry Adoption*. Bureau of Consular Affairs, US Department of State, n.d. Web. 12 Dec. 2013.

Chapter 5. Culture and Race

1. Amanda L. Baden, et al. "Reclaiming Culture: Reculturation of Transracial and International Adoptees." *Journal of Counseling & Development* 90.4 (Oct 2012): 387. *Expanded Academic ASAP (Gale)*. Web. 12 Dec. 2013.

2. Jena Martin. "The Good, The Bad, and The Ugly: The New Way of Looking at the Intercountry Adoption Debate (pdf)." *UC Davis Journal of International Law and Policy*. Regents of the University of California, 14 May 2007. Web. 12 Dec. 2013.

3. Nam Soon Huh and William J. Reid. "Intercountry, Transracial Adoption, and Ethnic Identity." *International Social Work* 43.1. Sage: London, 2000. *EBSCO Host*. Web. 13 Dec. 2013.

4. "Transcultural Adoption: Preparing for Special Changes." *Children's Home Society and Family Services*. CHSFS, 2013. Web. 13 Dec. 2013. 190–191.

5. Nicole Callahan. "Adoption Advocate No. 38: Race and Identity in Transracial Adoption: Suggestions for Adoptive Parents." *National Council for Adoption*. NCFA, 2011. Web. 12 Dec. 2013.

6. "Report Criticizes 'Colorblind' Adoptions." *NPR*. NPR, 27 May 2008. Web. 12 Dec. 2013.

SOURCE NOTES CONTINUED

7. Nicole Callahan. "Adoption Advocate No. 38: Race and Identity in Transracial Adoption: Suggestions for Adoptive Parents." *National Council for Adoption*. NCFA, 2011. Web. 12 Dec. 2013.

8. Jini L. Roby and Stacey A. Shaw. "The African Orphan Crisis and International Adoption." *Social Work* 51.3 (2006): 203. *Expanded Academic ASAP (Gale)*. Web. 13 Dec. 2013.

9. Jane Jeong Trenka, et al., eds. *Outsiders Within: Writing on Transracial Adoption*. Cambridge, MA: South End, 2006. Print. 10.

10. Nicole Callahan. "Adoption Advocate No. 38: Race and Identity in Transracial Adoption: Suggestions for Adoptive Parents." *National Council for Adoption*. NCFA, 2011. Web. 12 Dec. 2013.

11. Ibid.

12. "Convention on the Rights of the Child." *United National Human Rights*. Office of the High Commissioner for Human Rights, 2012. Web. 12 Dec. 2013.

Chapter 6. Institutions, Human Rights, and Health

1. Stephanie Pappas. "Early Neglect Alters Kids' Brains." *LiveScience*. LiveScience, 23 Jul. 2012. Web. 12 Dec. 2013.

2. Susan H. Lin, et al. "The Relation between Length of Institutionalization and Sensory Integration in Children Adopted from Eastern Europe." *American Journal of Occupational Therapy* 59.2 (Mar.–Apr. 2005): 139. *Expanded Academic ASAP (Gale)*. Web. 8 Dec. 2013.

3. Sara Dillon. "Making Legal Regimes for Intercountry Adoption Reflect Human Rights Principles." *Boston University International Law Journal* (Fall 2003): 5. *EBSCO Host*. Web. 13 Dec. 2013.

4. Chuck Johnson. "Emphasizing Family, Embracing Culture." *National Council for Adoption: Blog*. NCFA, 7 June 2012. Web. 15 Dec. 2013.

Chapter 7. Re-Homing and Abuse

1. Diane Clehane. "US Mother Who 'Returned' Her Adopted Son to Russia Ordered to Pay Child Support." *Forbes*. Forbes, 31 May 2012. Web. 8 Nov. 2013.

2. Damien Cave. "In Tenn., Reminders of a Boy Returned to Russia." *New York Times*. New York Times, 10 Apr. 2010. Web. 8 Nov. 2013.

3. Will Stewart. "Fury as US Woman Adopts Russian Boy, 7, Then Sends Him Back Alone." *MailOnline*. Associated Newspapers, 9 Apr. 2010. Web. 10 Nov. 2013.

4. "US Mother Who Sent Adopted Son, 7, Back to His Native Russia Alone Sued for Child Support." *MailOnline*. Associated Newspapers, 7 Mar. 2012. Web. 10 Nov. 2013

5. Laird Harrison. "International Adoptees Have Growing List of Medical Issues." *Family Practice News* 40.20 (1 Dec. 2010): 1. *Expanded Academic ASAP (Gale)*. Web. 6 Dec. 2013.

6. Ellen Pinderhughes, et al. "A Changing World: Shaping Best Practices through Understanding of the New Realities of Intercountry Adoption." *Evan B. Donaldson Adoption Institute*. Donaldson Adoption Institute, Oct. 2013. Web. 15 Dec. 2013.

7. Nicholas D. Kristof. "When Children Are Traded." *New York Times: Opinion Pages*. New York Times, 20 Nov. 2013. Web. 13 Dec. 2013.

8. Ibid.

9. Megan Twohey. "The Child Exchange." *Reuters Investigates*. Thomsonreuters.com, 9 Sept. 2013. Web. 15 Dec. 2013.

10. Ibid.

11. Megan Twohey. "Adoption Bulletin Board Monitors Provided No Oversight." *Milwaukee-Wisconsin Journal Sentinel*. Journal Sentinel, 10 Sept. 2013. Web. 15 Dec. 2013.

12. Megan Twohey. "The Child Exchange." *Reuters Investigates*. Thomsonreuters.com, 9 Sept. 2013. Web. 15 Dec. 2013.

13. Sarah Netter. "Tennessee Mother Ships Adopted Son Back to Moscow Alone." *ABC News*. ABC News Internet Ventures, 9 Apr. 2010. Web. 15 Dec. 2013.

14. Mikhail Metzel. "Death of Texas Toddler Fuels Russian Government Anti-Adoption Stance." *CBS News*. CBS News, 18 Feb. 2013. Web. 15 Dec. 2013.

15. David Crary. "Russian Adoption Ban: One Year Later." *Christian Science Monitor*. Christian Science Monitor, 18 Jan. 2014. Web. 19 Jan. 2014.

16. Sharon Worcester. "Meeting the Behavioral and Medical Needs of Foreign Adoptees." *Family Practice News*. 32.11 (1 June 2002): 46. *Expanded Academic ASAP (Gale)*. Web. 7 Dec. 2013.

Chapter 8. International Adoption Today

1. Sharon Jayson. "International Adoptions: Kids Older, Have Special Needs." *USA Today*. Gannett, 30 Oct. 2013. Web. 30 Oct. 2013.

2. Adam Pertman and Ellen Pinderhughes. "Eye-Opening Insights into International Adoption, Orphans, Special Needs and 'Re-homing.'" *HuffPost: Impact*. TheHuffingtonPost.com, 30 Oct. 2013. Web. 30 Oct. 2013.

3. Ellen Pinderhughes, et al. "A Changing World: Shaping Best Practices through Understanding of the New Realities of Intercountry Adoption." *Evan B. Donaldson Adoption Institute*. Donaldson Adoption Institute, Oct. 2013. Web. 15 Dec. 2013. 7.

4. Sharon Jayson. "International Adoptions: Kids Older, Have Special Needs." *USA Today*. Gannett, 30 Oct. 2013. Web. 30 Oct. 2013.

5. Ellen Pinderhughes, et al. "A Changing World: Shaping Best Practices through Understanding of the New Realities of Intercountry Adoption." *Evan B. Donaldson Adoption Institute*. Donaldson Adoption Institute, Oct. 2013. Web. 15 Dec. 2013. 11.

6. Judith Masson. "Intercountry Adoption: A Global Problem or a Global Solution?" *Journal of International Affairs* 55.1 (Fall 2001): 142. *EBSCO Host*. Web. 12 Dec. 2013.

7. Kathryn Joyce. *The Child Catchers: Rescue, Trafficking, and the New Gospel of Adoption*. Jackson, TN: PublicAffairs-Perseus, 2013. Print. 221.

8. Ibid.

9. Sarah Netter. "Tennessee Mother Ships Adopted Son Back to Moscow Alone." *ABC News*. ABC News Internet Ventures, 9 Apr. 2010. Web. 15 Dec. 2013.

10. E. J. Graff. "The Lie We Love." Foreign Policy. *Foreign Policy*, 10 Sep. 2010. Web. 12 Dec. 2013.

11. Ibid.

12. Ellen Pinderhughes, et al. "A Changing World: Shaping Best Practices through Understanding of the New Realities of Intercountry Adoption." *Evan B. Donaldson Adoption Institute*. Donaldson Adoption Institute, Oct. 2013. Web. 15 Dec. 2013. 8.

13. Peter Selman. "Global Trends in Intercountry Adoption: 2001–2010." *Adoption Advocate* 44 (Feb. 2012): 15–16. *Expanded Academic ASAP (Gale)*. Web. 10 Dec. 2013.

14. Ellen Pinderhughes, et al. "A Changing World: Shaping Best Practices through Understanding of the New Realities of Intercountry Adoption." *Evan B. Donaldson Adoption Institute*. Donaldson Adoption Institute, Oct. 2013. Web. 15 Dec. 2013.

INDEX

ABOUT THE AUTHOR

Rebecca Felix is a writer and editor from Minnesota. She has a bachelor of arts degree in English from the University of Minnesota–Twin Cities. Rebecca has written and edited numerous books for children and young adults on a variety of topics. These topics include exploration, genetics, energy alternatives and conservation, civil rights, and social issues.